THE END OF DREAMS

Floyd Skloot

THE END *of* DREAMS

poems

LOUISIANA STATE UNIVERSITY PRESS

BATON ROUGE

Published by Louisiana State University Press
Copyright © 2006 by Floyd Skloot
All rights reserved
Manufactured in the United States of America
FIRST PRINTING

DESIGNER: Michelle A. Garrod
TYPEFACE: Minion Pro, Roxy
PRINTER AND BINDER: Edwards Brothers, Inc.

LIBRARY OF CONGRESS CATALOGING-IN-PUBLICATION DATA

Skloot, Floyd.
  The end of dreams : poems / Floyd Skloot.
      p. cm.
  ISBN 0-8071-3116-4 (alk. paper) — ISBN 0-8071-3117-2 (pbk. : alk. paper)
  I. Title.
PS3569.K577E53 2006
811'.54—dc22

                                                          2005011575

These poems were previously published in the following journals: *AGNI*: "Feast of the Trumpets, Warsaw, 1884"; *Boulevard*: "Dowsing for Joy," "Eliot in the Afternoon," and "Night Wind"; *Colorado Review*: "The Train"; *Georgia Review*: "Whitman Pinch Hits, 1861"; *Hotel Amerika*: "Dry Spell"; *Hudson Review*: "Heritage" and "Kansas, 1973"; *Iowa Review*: "Light Wind" and "Rendezvous at Auvers, 1873"; *Leviathan Quarterly* (England): "The End of Dreams" and "The Flask"; *New Criterion*: "Dialysis"; *New Letters*: "Doomsday Drill"; *Ohio Review*: "Breath"; *Poet & Critic*: "The Ambassador Apartments"; *Poetry*: "Private Room"; *Poetry Ireland Review*: "The Dance" and "Light Wind"; *Poetry Northwest*: "A Hand of Casino, 1954," "O'Connor at Andalusia, 1964," and "Poolside"; *Prairie Schooner*: "Bach at Dusk"; *Sewanee Review*: "The End of Dreams"; *The Shop* (Ireland): "The Ambassador Apartments" and "Latin Lessons"; *Southern Review*: "The Flask," "The Hermit Thrush," "Nabokov, Mist," "Pontoise, 1887," and "Raoul Dufy at Fenway Park, 1950"; *Southern Poetry Review*: "A Quiet Light"; *Thumbscrew* (England): "A Hand of Casino, 1954" and "Dry Spell"; *Tikkun*: "Lost Psalm"; *Tracks* (Ireland): "The Fall Term"; *Valparaiso Poetry Review*: "The Moonlight Manuscript, 1696"; *Virginia Quarterly Review*: "The Dance"; *Willow Review*: "The Fall Term"; *Yankee*: "Openings."
  "The End of Dreams," "O'Connor at Andalusia, 1964," and "Poolside" were reprinted in *JAMA: The Journal of the American Medical Association*.
  "Openings" appeared in the chapbook *Poppies* (Eugene, OR: Silverfish Review Press / Story Line Press, 1994). Thanks to its editor, Rodger Moody.
  The Heinrich Böll Foundation (Achill Island, Ireland) provided a writing residency during the time some of these poems were lived or written. My thanks to John F. Deane, who at the time was director of the Heinrich Böll Foundation in Ireland. I also wish to thank the Oregon Arts Commission for an Individual Artist Fellowship, and Oregon Literary Arts Inc. for the William Stafford Fellowship in Poetry.
  For their inspiration, encouragement, or commentary, my gratitude goes to Robert Gibb, Beverly Hallberg, Lawrence B. Salander, Rebecca Skloot, Ron Slate, and Dabney Stuart.

The paper in this book meets the guidelines for permanence and durability of the Committee on Production Guidelines for Book Longevity of the Council on Library Resources. ∞

For Beverly

He said that everything possessed
The power to transform itself, or else,

And what meant more, to be transformed.
   —WALLACE STEVENS, "Two Illustrations That the World Is What You Make of It"

CONTENTS

I.

The past is but the beginning of a beginning,
and all that is and has been is but the twilight of the dawn.
—H. G. WELLS, *The Discovery of the Future*

A HAND OF CASINO, 1954

My grandfather studies the cards.
His jaw juts and he begins to shift
the pink plate of his false teeth,
tonguing it out and in, mouth
widening till his grin has flipped
upside-down between the gums.
He slams a deuce onto the table.

Even at seven I know he is losing
on purpose. He mumbles deep
in his throat, a gargle of sounds
like someone choking on stones.
I think he would make sense
if his teeth were put in right.

At seven I also know that bodies
crumble but new parts can come
gleaming from dark hiding places.
I have seen, buried at the back
of his top drawer, my father's spare
glass eye in a navy velvet box.
My mother has three heads
of stiff hair inside her closet,
just in case, and a secret pack
of fingernails in her chiffonier.

My grandfather strings phrases
of Polish and Yiddish around words
in French to hold his broken
English together. I understand
nothing he says but everything
that is in his eyes. He tells me
he is *a man from the world.*
That must be where he learned
that losing is winning as a frown

is a smile and a curse is a kiss.
When I lay down the good
deuce, he smacks his furrowed
brow and curses high heaven.

DOOMSDAY DRILL

Brooklyn, N.Y., 1953

Sirens blared as my father rose in the dead
of night like a dream. The dome of his white
helmet gleamed where our hall light struck it.
One arm, circled by a civil defense band,
gripped a glowing yellow Geiger counter
to his hip. I knew what to do. He yawned
and the sound of alarm seemed to come
from somewhere deep inside as I dressed.
Face solemn without its cigar, he led us
from the apartment into a calm sea
of neighbors flowing down to shelter
in the cellar. They parted to let him
through and followed him into a dark
room where the whole world changed.
Moonlight erupted through the barred
window above our heads. My mother
sat silent against the wall, a towel spread
to protect her from dirt. Mr. Brown
from the floor above us pacing a circle
in plaid pajamas and Panama hat embraced
his spaniel. Mrs. Honig wore a torn robe
with galoshes and her hulking son Henry
whimpered as he hid his eyes in her arms.
My father with stopwatch and flashlight
stood by the door beneath a sign that said
IT CAN HAPPEN HERE. Among the chained
bicycles, Flexible Flyers and stacked boxes
of winter clothes I saw darkness become
safety, warmth become wisdom, and silence
the fallout of everyone's secret fear.

POOLSIDE

There is less than one hour left
and my father does not know.
He lies there in faded light
green trunks, turned belly-up
beneath a livid sunlamp,
chewing his last stick of Dentyne
before the time comes
for him to rise and dress.
He loves the sheer arrogance
of such heat, its dragon's
breath across his chest,
and he fills his lungs with it.

Minutes remain but still
he does not know. He thinks
of the long morning spent
riding bridle paths on a bay
gelding, the mid-day nap,
pinochle on a sun-drenched
patio and whiskey as clouds
turned his bright day dark
in the blink of an eye.
He thinks of tomorrow only
as a long drive home.

Seconds more as he rises
to stretch and blink salt
from his eyes. He does not
know yet. Without the least
thought of time winding down,
he tucks glasses in a towel
on the lounger and strides
across the deck as though
it were nothing. He breathes,
flexes his toes over the edge,
dives into the cool embrace
of deep water and dies.

THE AMBASSADOR APARTMENTS

Its brick face weathered by salt air and spray,
The Ambassador sagging towards land's end
is the last place my grandparents will stay
together. Wind flaps the shredded awning
below their thin windows every morning
and drives him from the room. He wants to mend

it like the torn sable pelts and tattered
linings he mended for fifty-five years.
It is not the noise. Noise never mattered
to him, surrounded all day by sewing
machines, cutters, fans. It is not knowing
what it will sound like when the thing he fears

most starts to happen, though he thinks it will
sound like this. It will wake him so he can
see her spirit leave its mark on the sill,
grains of sand whirling skyward. It will call
him back from dreams of Cracow in the fall
dusk, a Chopin polonaise, the young man

and woman—she is so small beside him—
sitting on a marble bench waiting for
the full moon. He will arise in the dim
light of their last years, hear the rattling glass,
and know without looking what came to pass
in the night. He has heard it all before.

KANSAS, 1973

My daughter nestled in a plastic seat
is nodding beside me as though in full
agreement with the logic of her dream.
I am glad for her sake the road is straight.
But the dark shimmer of a summer road
where hope and disappointment repeat
themselves all across Kansas like a dull
chorus makes the westward journey seem
itself a dream. She breathes in one great
gulp, taking deep the blazing air, and stops
my heart until she sighs the breath away.
The sun is stuck directly overhead.

I thought it all would never end. The drive,
the heat, my child beside me, the bright day
itself, that fathering time in my life.
We were going nowhere and never would,
as in a dream, or in the space between
time and memory. I saw nothing but sky
beyond the horizon of still treetops
and nothing changing down the road ahead.

DIALYSIS

In my brother's blind and dying
eyes I was forever young.
He rocked and slept to the sound
of my voice as long as memory
played its tune. Then he woke
to speak of vast silver platters
heaped with meat and bouquets
of cheese, hot loaves the way
we found them on the island.
He said my breath had carried
the dream along. We were back
to back again in the Valiant's
front seat, doors gaping and feet
on the seething summer streets
of Flatbush. As his eyes closed
and sullied blood spun in loops
of plastic tubing, I watched
my brother closing down his life.
Time fell apart in his mind,
leaving nowhere but the past
for him to live. His will to sit
through this ritual cleansing
weakened as each day blended
until only sleep remained.

PRIVATE ROOM

His mother has let go
of the past. She floats
on the surface of time,
her hands describing
slow circles in the air.
Gazing down the dark
dimensions of her ninety
years, she is content
at last to be alive.
She watches him hover,
hoping to scavenge
the bones of her memories
for one final morsel.
In her vast eyes he finds
only his own poised
and gleaming talons.

THE FLASK

Behind glass in my daughter's dining room,
the cracked leather flaps of my father's flask
dangled from its shoulders like unfastened
suspenders. By candlelight I saw the oval
sixty-year-old stain still centered on its plaid
coat in the place where a heart would be.
As we passed, hands filled with steaming bowls
of *Tortellini in Brodo,* the dented metal cap
my father used to measure shots of rye held
our faces for an instant like flashes of memory.

Now I am the child and he is alive. It is another
November night, his face grim in the glass
as he ties and reties his Windsor knot, bracing
himself with a swig from the flask for the dark
task ahead. In a blink of the eye we are inside
a dining room, strange people passing behind
me, smiling as they speak of my father's Kosher
chicken market, now theirs, and I watch hands
filled with steaming bowls of *Tortellini in Brodo*
set them down so that the scent fills my head
and lifts me into the autumn sky until nothing

made sense for a moment except my daughter
as she sat across from me, smiling at her groom,
turning to smile at me, her face slowly masked
by the steam that rose like the past made whole.

HERITAGE

These pink pills I hold in my palm
might have saved my father's life.

Insubstantial as tears, dust of fungus
pressed and formed into small shields,

they would have kept his heart open
for years to a full flow of blood.

But he felt nothing that said danger
hid in the mass of his chambers

and valves, so he did nothing but live
as his own father had lived and died.

Now I take one each night before sleep.
In the last week he has been returning

to me in dreams, always moving away
from the light, as though my reaching

the age he was at death freed him
at last to seek a final place of rest.

II.

BREATH

I weighed about 130 pounds, and I just had to grow a little more.
I did lots of exercises. I did running and that kind of stuff.
   —FRANK SINATRA

For depth of breath young Sinatra
like a boxer ran five morning miles.
Solo on the high school track, thin
as the stripe on a lane, he was all
ears, all bone. He was all business.

The first laps were always for love
songs, nice and easy till he found
his rhythm, drawing the urban air
in deep. The moment he became
one with wind, he knew the way
a body held in check could move
exactly like a melody. It was simple
as swimming underwater. His stride
grew smooth, fingers to shoulders
to hips to toes, graceful as a smile
across low notes as the key shifted.

That was for the long lines of lyric
no one else could hold. In time he ran
for the uptempo tunes, let go a little
to get the torso involved and bring
his thin arms into play, his gait all glissando.
Step by step he swelled from the inside
out, making himself strong enough
for song. He ran past pain, timed by
the beat of his heart because song
was not about how fast but how long.
This was his Golden Age, Jersey City
in the early Thirties, his moment to make
dreams come true. Music was in the air.
He knew he could go on like that forever
because his dreams began with breath.

O'CONNOR AT ANDALUSIA, 1964

Sickness before death is a very appropriate thing and
I think those who don't have it miss one of God's mercies.
    —FLANNERY O'CONNOR, *The Habit of Being*

It came with the steady pace of dusk,
slow shadings in the distance, a sense of light
growing soft at the center of her body.
It came like evening to the farm
bearing silence and a promise of rest.
There was nothing to say it was there
till she found herself unable to move
and stillness settled its net over the bed.
A crimson disc of pain suddenly flushed
from her hips like a last flaring of sun.

She believed the time had come
to welcome this perfect weakness
that had no memory of strength,
a mercy even as darkness hardened
inside her joints. It was not to be
missed. Nor was the mercy of sight:
she believed the time had come
to measure every moment and map
the place she soon must leave.
At least she had been given time,
though her wish would have been
an hour more for each leaf visible
from her window, a day for trees,
a week for birds and month to savor
the voice of each friend who called.
Though she never belonged in the heart
of this world, she gave this world her heart.

Within her stillness she remembered
the first signs: that brilliant butterfly
rash on her face, a blink that lasted

for hours, the delicate embrace of sleep
veering as in a dream toward the grip
of death, hunger vanishing like hope.
Her body no longer knew her body as itself

but this too was a mercy. To leave herself
behind and then return was instructive.
To wax and wane, to live beyond
the body and know what that was like,
a gift from God, a mixed blessing shrouded
in the common cloth of loss. Half her life
she practiced death and resurrection.

WHITMAN PINCH HITS, 1861

After six months of wandering Whitman found himself
at the edge of a Long Island potato farm in early fall.
He saw a squad of young men at sport on sparse grass.
Looking up, he saw a few stray geese rise and circle back
north as though confused by the sudden Indian summer,
then looked down to study cart tracks cut deep into mud.
Weary of his own company, shorn of appetite, he thought
it would be sweet to sit awhile beside this field and watch
the boys in their shabby flannel uniforms playing ball.
Caught between wanting to look at them and wanting
them to look at him, he could not tell from this distance
if the torn and faded blues they wore were soldiers' clothes
or baseball clothes. But he loved the rakish tilt of their caps
and cocky chatter drifting on the mid-day air. He had seen
the game played before, in Brooklyn, on a pebbled patch
laid out beside the sea, and thought it something young,
something brotherly for the frisky young and their brothers
to do in the shadow of civil war. That seemed two lifetimes
ago, not two years. The face he could no longer bear to find
in a mirror looked now like this island's ploughed ground.
Time does turn thick, Whitman thought, does press itself
against a man's body as he moves through a world torn apart
by artillery fire and weeping. Without knowing it happened,

he settled on a rise behind the makeshift home, moving
as he moved all year, a ghost in his own life. He should write
about baseball for the *Eagle,* or better still, make an epic poem
of it. The diamond chalked on grass, stillness held in a steady
light before the burst of movement, boys with their faces open
to the sky as a struck ball rose toward the all-consuming clouds.
But it was the sound that held him rapt. Wild, musical voices
punctuated by a pock of bat on ball, then the dropped wood
clattering to earth, grunts, everyone in motion through the air,
the resistant air, and then the lovely laughter. Whitman laughed
with them, a soundless gargle. The next batter staggered and fell,
drunk, his chin tobacco-splattered, laughing at his own antics

as he limped back to the felled tree where teammates sat.
They shook their heads, ignoring the turned ankle he exposed
for them to admire. Suddenly all eyes turned toward Whitman

where he lounged, propped on one elbow, straw hat tilted
to keep the sun from his neck, on the hill that let him see
everything at once. They beckoned. They needed Whitman
to pinch hit, to keep the game going into its final inning.
The injured batter held his stick out, thick end gripped in his fist,
and barked a curse. Whitman sat up, the watcher summoned
into a scene he has forgotten he did not create. They beckoned
and he came toward them like a bather moving through
thigh-high breakers, time stopping and then turning back,
letting him loose at last amid the spirits that greeted him
as the boys pounded his back, as they turned him around
and shoved him toward the field. In his hands, the wood
felt light. He stood beside the folded coat that represented
home, shifted his weight and stared at the pitcher who glared
back, squinting against the sun, taking the poet's measure.

RENDEZVOUS AT AUVERS, 1873

Cézanne alone among the stone huts longs
for light to hold still. He hears the river
and wind within the chestnut trees as songs
in discordant keys that come together

with the rustle of distant wheat and all
he wants to do now is curse high heaven.
Color swirls before his eyes, thick, a brawl
of values. He has wandered for seven

hours waiting for Pissarro to arrive
from Paris, soil blackening, air turning
ocher, the landscape no longer alive
along its sage folds. He has been learning

green and gold, the use of blue, softer strokes
like the caught breath of vision. But he needs
Pissarro to calm him before rage chokes
the last hope of brightness. Cézanne concedes

nothing to the sudden cold front or shift
in shadows, slathering paint in layers
to approximate morning's sullen drift
toward blue. Then, like an answer to his prayers,

footsteps through the hillside grasses, the clink
of wine bottles, a murmur of leather
easel straps loosened and long sighs like zinc
white skies the moment they are together.

PONTOISE, 1887

She is frightened this year will be his last.
Always paint flecks mottle his hair and brows,
fill the deep ruts of his skin, stain his clothes.
Paint turns his tongue blue. His eyes are a shade
of hazel they have never been before
and their exhausted glare makes her afraid
to see herself reflected there anymore.
She smells where he stood to paint pastured cows.
She hears his shallow rasp of breath and knows
he has done himself harm again, smoked all
day, drunk cheap claret from that filthy cup
he straps to his palette. It is late fall,
cold even in the sun, but he has been up
since dawn in search of the river's first light
as it lets go of clouds. He tramped the banks,
then shared his loaf with peasant girls in bright
kerchiefs, lingering to watch the broken ranks
of red roofs come back to life as time passed.

THE MOONLIGHT MANUSCRIPT, 1696

1. Johann Christopf Bach

I heard my brother drifting through the night.
But I did nothing. I believed it was only
a dream, little more than my own fears
given form by troubled sleep. Ghosts,
I thought, do not move so idly, even the green
ghosts of one's parents. But I did nothing.

When our mother died I prayed our father
would marry. Within the year he did.
For a time, then, I was free to worry about
keeping the people of St. Michael in song,
and my own first son breathing the sweet
air of Ohrdruf. Back in Eisenach, I heard,
my young brothers thrived in their new
family, their home again always in song.

But before another year passed, as though
choked by thwarted mourning, father joined
our mother once more. And my brothers were
with me. Jacob soon left, a man already
at fourteen, and day by day Sebastian sank
further into silence. He was only ten when
I heard him become a spirit of the night.

Turning back to my wife's soft form,
I sought to forget those shadowy sounds.
Come morning, I found myself caught
again in the snares of work and prayer,
burdened as I was by choirs to conduct,
students to teach, hospital and castle
chapels to serve, two shabby organs
to tend and holiday melodies to compose.

2. *Johann Sebastian Bach*

I was lost until the music found me
where I wandered the timeless night,
drawn to my brother's grillwork cabinet only
to see those manuscripts lit by moonlight.
But seeing was not enough. I was lost
until the music found me and how could
I leave it there? As in a dream I crossed
a rush of moonlight softening the wood
floor and drifted close. It was there. I thought
if I could copy what my brother had
copied, then the music would not be lost
as my parents had been lost. I was glad
to save the music that was saving me
note by note, melody by melody.

3. *Johann Christopf Bach*

Spring mornings I heard Sebastian humming
familiar melodies. The soft sound baffled me
at first, like a breeze made song. I was pleased
to see my brother smile. My wife's glance
was pure joy since the boy was growing so
light. As April worked its way toward May,
I began to recognize Sebastian's repertoire.
He was humming a measure from Froberger!

The only place Sebastian could have come
to know the tune was in my grillwork cabinet,
the book of clavier pieces copied as instruction
from my teacher Pachelbel. Rare pieces by Kerll
and Krieger, Nivers and Witt. I saw nothing
was missing there, but feared a second copy
would spoil the value of my own. Sebastian

was not himself in this deed and I mourned
the need to discipline a deeply grieving child.
Besides, I had grown used to his fugue of night
noises. Yet I knew I must lock the book away.
It was mine to protect, as Sebastian was mine
to protect, and the curled edges of delicate
paper exposed his secret as clearly as the music
coming from his mouth. What would he learn
of life if I failed to punish willful disobedience?

It broke my heart to hear him silent once
again, unwilling even to sing in the choir.
He tinkered with the broken organ pipes
and pedals, but denied the town his sweet

soprano voice. I thought to give him time.
I thought he would be unable to bear a life
without music giving form to all he lost.

4. Johann Sebastian Bach

It did not matter where the music went.
Moonlight, and notes in their field of clear white
space, melodies filling the mind and heart
as time and heavenly light filled the night
sky, until I knew nothing would be lost.
As long as music floated like the ghost
of faith in the air around me I might
be safe. I would go where the music went.

FEAST OF THE TRUMPETS, WARSAW, 1884

The plume of a steam train crossing
the Vistula mixes with thick cumulus.
Dark smoke from dockside shacks
and warehouses gathers like a sail
in the wind. On the bank, open fires
smudge the near surface of the river.

Oblivious of all that will soon engulf
them, a scattered dozen bearded
men pray and chant in the new year's
first dawning. Dressed in black
caftans, each swaying man is facing
a different direction, as though God
were everywhere and prayer the sole
purpose of their being in the world.

Some have empty hands folded behind
their backs, eyes toward heaven
and the absent sun's shining. Others hold
holy books open, or their naked palms
up, or hands clasped before their hearts.

Beside the fire, dressed in white,
one peasant balancing a bucket
on his hip stares at the worshipers.
Ready to feed another scrap of wood
to the fire, a friend squats at his feet
and listens to something: Whispers,
perhaps, from the man in white,
the hiss of rising flame, lapping river
water or the train's sudden whistle.

RAOUL DUFY AT FENWAY PARK, 1950

1. The Letter

Dr. Homburger at his desk in Boston
rocks in place and feels the cool face
of a stethoscope tapping his chest.
He gazes down at a magazine photo
in which Raoul Dufy sits at his tilted
desk in Montmartre. All Homburger
can see is the painter's warped hand
like a claw grappling his narrow brush.

The light is bad, but he knows the art
well enough to have noticed Dufy's
giddy flowers shrinking on their stems
year by year. Now he sees those hands
have been blooming with pain as well.

He looks away, allows a brief distraction
as morning sunlight winks off a sculler's
gleaming oars. Some days Homburger
would trade all he owns to see water
shimmer as Dufy has seen it, or feel
the depth of such blue as it ranges
through to joy. But then to lose all that!

The way Dufy's bouquets once burst
into smile. That implication of breeze
where threshers labored as a storm
gathered, or the lazy curves of a violin
at rest upon a rococo yellow console.
Homburger pushes aside the magazine
and centers a sheet of paper on his blotter.
He gathers himself and writes: *My Dear Dufy.*

2. The Treatment

Homburger thinks Dufy cannot be this
old man setting crutches aside as he sits
where afternoon light cannot reach.
He finally understands those stark black
paintings Dufy has done of late, men
frozen in place while a bull gathers strength,
figures etched against a sky dark enough
to stop the heart. The men have talked all
day, a collage of languages saying *hope*
and *help* till nothing remains but this
lifted syringe. For one instant, it points
toward skies that are a color Dufy has never
encountered before, then lets loose a drip
he sees as pure faith. It enters skin that
always feels afire. There is only more pain.

Dufy has not wanted to hear the name
of these new hormones, placing a tumid
finger across the doctor's lips whenever
Homburger speaks of them. *Cortisone.*
ACTH. No, he wants to feel their colors
rush, if he can, and looks away to find again
the memory of young sunbathers lounging
on pink and saffron blankets by the Charles.

3. The Game

Dufy crosses his room the way he imagines
snowmelt crosses rocks where a river is born.
He flicks a sable brush against his open palm
and looks through a stack of quick sketches,
flowers that bloomed as his fingers shrank

almost before his eyes. Within three days
he has gotten back his hands. The knock
of knuckles on his door like a throat clearing,
then Homburger is beside him at the open
window asking if there is anything he wants.

Twilight softens the air. The harbor waits
with arms open. *What more is there?*
In reply, the doctor fans a pair of tickets
to the Red Sox game and offers a royal
blue hat crowned with the team's red B.

Under the lights, Dufy is dazzled as much
by being able to climb steps and hold
a hot dog in his hand as by the delicate
dance of Dom DiMaggio under a fly
to deep centerfield. A woman seated
before Dufy wears a red rose in her hair
and drinks beer the color of summer

light above the harbor at Deauville.
Even the names afloat on the night
are blessings to his ear: *Dropo, Zarilla.*
When the crowd rises for a Williams
line drive, Dufy is up with them, laughing,
clapping his hands as the sound spirals
like a spray of anemones from their vase.

III.

And what remains when disbelief has gone?
—PHILIP LARKIN, "Church Going"

A QUIET LIGHT

A light he was to no one but himself
Where now he sat, concerned with he knew what,
A quiet light, and then not even that.
    —ROBERT FROST, "An Old Man's Winter Night"

A thick woolen sweater and cedar fire
on nights this hot tell you as much about
my health now as the doctor's fancy chart.
Call it one long inner winter in high
summer, the northern sort that knows no light.
I never spoke of what was going on
inside each breath and then it was too late.
Metastasis. Now a fire soothes but I
cannot abide its flickers on my eyes.
I am alone and waiting at land's end,
where either the tides have ceased or I have
lost the last of my hearing. I tremble
and tingle within my brain's wild sparkings.

My silences were never about pain,
only the memory of pain. I lived
a kind of twilight sleep until there was
no pain to remember, thinking I could
always outlast the worst. Refuse to pay
attention and the need to attend would
pass like stillness between beats of a heart,
like a new moon's dark glare. It was the same
with fear; I know that now. And doubt, and loss.
But drowning on air is hard to ignore.
The frenzied grip of cells gone crazy all
throughout the body is hard to ignore.

It is easier if I close my eyes.
The dreamy ricochet of shadows frees
my mind and sometimes brings a moment's ease.
But then disembodied cries of children

combing the beach for shells seem to reach me
across a space defined by wind and time.
I think of the long afterlife of stars,
a burst of light that is pure memory,

the past made present by a trick of air,
so that what we see has been dead for years.
Next comes the scent of stranded kelp saying
there is no stronghold where the sea floor shifts.

Burning cedar is the odor of fall,
always has been, but I will never see
another fall. Here the leaves do not lose
their green anyway, nor the land its grip
on life. Wherever I turn now, there is
no rest from growth. I am aware I have
run out of time. Dear Lord, it has been so
long and I have drifted so far from home.
I fear you no longer remember me.

LIGHT WIND

The wind is light and smells of summer rain.
He lies beneath his years, adrift in light,
cooled by wind. The morphine taken for pain
has left him in a pillowed daze. Where night

is caught by day, where light and shadow catch
as wind ruffles cedar and sugar pine,
he thinks he hears rain. In a tear-drop patch
of light across his chest he can count nine

faces he remembers. Then it turns dark
and the faces catch like tufts of cotton
on the ragged fence of his toes. They mark
his body's end. Now he has forgotten

everything but the smell of summer rain
mingled with cedar and sugar pine. Light
it seems can be borne on wind the way pain
can be borne on breath, or a trace of night

on noon's brilliant shimmer. The wind is light.
The wind is summer rain, the breath of years,
a face transformed to memory. The night
has come at last to wash away his tears.

Gone now, leaving only light. Gone, as pain
is gone, and time, and then the sound of rain.

LOST PSALM

God was the clear pane at the heart
of a stained glass burning bush
filling the temple's western wall.

God was water when I walked
the beach during the eye
of a hurricane. God was water
swelling as the storm moved
across land and then was
the storm in full force.
God was a dune risen
to meet the surge and God
was a dune shrunk
to welcome winter wind.

God was on the tongue
of the first girl I kissed,
then God was on my tongue.

God spoke with flickering
light in a flood of sighs,
spoke without breath,
warm, spoke in tongues.

God was high in the stands
when I was knocked free
of time and space for one
full week making a tackle
in the open field. I shook
on the ground as if charged
by His light. All next spring
and early summer, God sped
through cycles of color
just beyond the edge of sight.

Doctors named it an aftereffect
of trauma but I understood it
was the afterglow of grace
and for months God could be
glimpsed in the creases of dream,
heard just beyond the bell buoy

at land's end, felt in spindrift
when the moon was full.

Finally God was in eastern
Pennsylvania, looming in books
and seminars. But somewhere
on the Susquehanna near Safe Harbor,
crewing a Flying Dutchman,
stretched out to my fullest
over the rushing river
in an effort to keep us all afloat,
I lost Him in a sudden luff of wind.

THE TRAIN

To get there you have to take the first train
you see and forget about direction.
There is no schedule on which to depend
so forget about time. Sit with your back
turned to whatever comes along the track
and be sure to notice how the thin chain
of daylight unravels its connection
with a night you believed would never end.

Since there is no moment when the chain snaps,
there is no moment when you know for sure
you are lost. Mountains with snow on their caps
suggest how far you have come to capture
the knowledge that there is nothing to gain
from asking where you are. No one is there
to answer. You never know. Remember,
though, there is no such thing as the wrong train.

LATIN LESSONS

The daughter of the local florist taught
us Latin in the seventh grade. We sat
like hothouse flowers nodding in a mist
of conjugations, declining nouns that
made little sense and adjectives that missed
the point. She was elegant, shapely, taut.
She was dazzling and classic, a perfect
example to us of such absolute
adjectives as *unique* or *ideal* or *perfect.*
The room held light. Suffering from acute
puberty, we could still learn case by case
to translate with her from the ancient tongue
by looking past her body to the chaste
scribblings she left on the board. We were young
but knew that the ablative absolute
was not the last word in being a part
of something while feeling ourselves apart
from everything that mattered most. We chased
each other on the ballfield after class
though it did no good. What we caught was not
what we were after, no matter how fast
we ran. She first got sick in early fall.
A change in her voice, a flicker of pain
across her face, and nothing was the same.
She came back to us pale and more slender
than ever, a phantom orchid in strong
wind, correcting our pronoun and gender
agreement, verb tense, going over all
we had forgotten while she was gone. Long
before she left for good in early spring,
she made sure the dead language would remain
alive inside us like a buried spring.

NIGHT WIND

I woke to wind that rose
from far below the dawn.
It spoke of light as lost
for good, as dream only,
then died. Creeping thyme
ruffled the window screen,
letting its scent loose
in our room, lacing the air
with a deep taste of green.

If there were the bluebird's
soft flutings or scrub jay's
notes, I would have turned
myself over to the morning.
But all I heard were screech
owls' crazed whistles
that meant night was holding.
I felt time stretch and curl
itself back into the distance
from which wind rose again.

THE END OF DREAMS

He wakens knowing this to be the day
his hopeless singing voice at last will sound
exactly like the young Robert Goulet.
It is the day for him to touch the ground
as only noble Fred Astaire has done
before, and only once, and with someone

perfect in his arms. He will be able
to accompany himself on the grand
piano by sight, bass hand and treble
hand like swallows in flight, each magic hand
nimble and light as the air that trembles
with the music he will make at the end

of all his dreams. It feels simple and right
to draw in all the air he can, to grow
still, then soar. Now they all stand around
his bed, in tears, and he sees the pure light
that means the time has come for him to sound
the first note, take the first step, and let go.

IV.

So Good-luck came, and on my roofe did light,
    Like noyse-less Snow; or as the dew of night:
        Not all at once, but gently, as the trees
Are, by the Sun-beames, trickl'd by degrees.
      —ROBERT HERRICK, "The comming of good luck"

BACH AT DUSK

After clearing five years of blackberry
vines from the slope behind our hives,
we could see June light turning copper
again as it spread against the hill's crest.

At rest on the porch, we could feel time
slow as color rose and a honed moon
began to show above the Coast Range.
For five springs, too sick for this work,
I learned that woods reclaim any land
left on its own though nothing changed
while I watched.
                    Soon a pack of mule deer,
coats giving back the sun's glow, arrived
to scout the rubble. Their ears twitched
as they looked east, black tails flicking,
mouths suddenly stilled. Then they turned
together to bound through the ragged edge
of oak and pine.
                    Behind them, wig askew,
braces dangling, belly strewn with brambles,
Bach strolled into the new clearing, boot laces
loose, pale tongues flapping where sunlight
found them. Shadowed by leaves, he sat
on a stump and sighed, an old man fresh
from long sleep, sorting through dreams.

When he raised his arms as if to conduct
darkness down, a pair of dark-eyed juncos
trilled and darted for cover. The wind roused,
its sound a minor chord held in the highest
limbs. Like wood smoke trapped in mist,
light spread under the gathering darkness
drenched us with a scent of wild ginger.

All week, my wife had played Bach sonatas
on her violin. I wondered if this explained
his presence, but she played Strauss as well
and only Bach had come. Perhaps he was
a side effect of pain medicine, or an aurora
caused by fatigue and early evening clouds.
A revenant slipping through the filigree
of lost time.

                Now his blunt hands grew busy
about his body as he made things straight,
chins quivering when he breathed, composing
himself.

                Then he was ten feet away. Bent over
to study our small pond that would be drained
to scum by deer in mid-July, arms akimbo,
he seemed cross, and worse when he gazed
at our garden with its knotted crop of peas,
butter lettuce and spinach just beginning to yield,
its border of upheaved stones.

                      There is order
here, I wanted to say, form that imitates
the land's own layered folds, though its signature
key happens to escape me at the moment.

My wife placed a hand on my shoulder and smiled
at the movement of my eyes. She did not see
Bach but saw that I was lost in what our work
had opened up.

                I imagined the untangled land
would satisfy him. The strict discipline of evergreen
if he looked far enough south across the valley,
or an impromptu ballet of sparrows rotating
between teeming feeders. In the last five years
I came to see an order hidden all around here.

But he grew grimmer as he wandered over
the vista, like a teacher seeing only what we
had missed: stems that promised more vines;
oozing tips of poison oak; a scatter of eggshells,
old banana peels, rotten celery stalks and coffee
grounds where tossed compost missed its mark.
Chaos of waste and new growth.

Country life!

I thought I saw him smile. As he turned,
light leaped from his eyes. In his cupped hands,
a clump of Oregon iris, their lavender petals
drooping across both wrists like cuffs, leaves
dense enough to make rope when stripped
to their fibers.

    Iris tenax, the tenacious one,
rainbow of the eye, blooming in clusters
where the ground held onto its moisture.

Still smiling, eyes closed as he let the flowers
fall, Bach began fading even as I understood
him to say *You see?*

    A rhythm deep within
the woods, something like the pounding
of hooves, was carrying him away, beyond
the field, where light was all but gone.

THE DANCE

My wife is fiddling "Turkey in the Straw"
in softening summer light. As her feet
begin to shuffle of their own accord,
the air around her softens and the beat
takes hold. Music fills the round room she's in.
It circles her figure, then spirals down
the stairs. As if summoned by her tune, wind
stirs to whirl its way over and around
the lilies blooming in our yard. Swaying
cherry and oak that shade our bed in late
afternoon lose themselves in her playing
too. Now the dance is rippling in one great
wave through the breath of every living thing
here. There is nothing left to do but sing.

THE HERMIT THRUSH

Along the line of dawn a hermit
thrush sings down summer dark.
Breeze stirring oak leaves brings
a sweet odor of stargazer lilies
through our screen and now light
begins to find the room. Eyes shut,
I see the thrush flick its wings
and rusty tail, nervous as the woods
warp around him. Sky shifts in place,
restless with its promise of rain.

You built this house round and snug
to the ground like a nest among
gnarled second growth as if knowing
the time would come for me
to share it. Nothing ever fit me
like the shape of morning here.
I lie still against the curve
of your back as one last dream
produces a trill at the edge
of your breath, its rising phrases
woven into the songbird's spiral.

OPENINGS

Close enough to touch a sky given back
by the still surface, to catch the hopscotch
of dragonflies and one shadowy hawk
chasing a last shaft of sunlight, you watch
as young Comanche waterlilies fold
their yellow petals together. The night
tells them to hide their blooms in your pond's cold
heart till morning calls them to life with light.

Night-bloomer splotched sudden pink like the Pearl
of the Pool, you tell me your secret name
in return for mine. I can see the girl
christened Beautiful Lily as she came
alive by light of the moon. Nothing to
hide or fear. I too come open to you.

DRY SPELL

Day by day the well
dwindled, its water
rank with minerals
and harder than ever.
All night I heard
wind through parched
leaves as the score
for a dream of endless
sands. When I woke
the first summer rain
was bringing color back
to life. Lilies shivered
in the light of dawn
brushing my window.
A hummingbird
loud in its stillness
lingered over pearled
lamb's ear and wild
rosemary shrugged
open blue blossoms.
I knew it was all false
hope, but the morning
air was whispering
fall and it was possible
to imagine the leaves
letting go, no longer
needing to hoard water,
welcoming a burst
of red and gold before
abandoning themselves
to the grass for good.

ELIOT IN THE AFTERNOON

In the fourth year of drought,
in late September when our parched garden
was lost to spotted spurge and blackberry vine,
when only Russian sage and flannel bush thrived
in their tonsure of blonde grass near our bedroom
window and the fig stood cockeyed with heat,

I sat in a cracked Adirondack chair under twin fir,
occupying the daily zone between analgesic doses,
watching bees traffic around wild rosemary

and saw out of the corner of my eye Eliot show
himself beside our slowly dying well.
                                        At first
he was pooled light that burst into flame
and became a flare of wind-blown leaves
as I turned to look.
                        Though this light was soaked
up at once by swaying oak and box elder, I had time
to think: You won't need that umbrella here.

I did not remember seeing hallucinations
listed as a side effect of this drug, and with all signs
of him vanished I sat back to catch the frozen
dance of a rufous hummingbird above yarrow.

Then I noticed Eliot's bowler nestled in a fold
of land where we stacked deadfall for winter fires.
I stood, shading my eyes, and saw the hat
for what it was: a dented boulder half-emerged
from its niche, our customary seat at the nightly
Concerto for Water Dripping Into Near-Empty Tank,
in the key of Despair Minor.
                                He remained beyond reach,
a shape without mass in the space between trees,
but I knew he had come. All day, to pass the time,

I had been trying to reconcile the cycles
of my illness with the cycles of rainfall, the rise
and fall of temperature or barometer, phases
of moon, patterns of cloud. It seemed fit
that out of such fruitless brooding Eliot should
arrive, accompanied by the warbler's *twit twit twit,*
and decide not to *come too close.*
                                        I believed it
best to be still, as with a spooked cat, and let
him join all us *creatures of the summer heat.*

Should I call him Tom or Mr. Eliot?
Should I ask him to sit with me in the shade?
Should I offer him a peach?

I must have slept, because sky was going silver
with vague cirrus when I saw him move across
the gravel drive. He had found a deer trail
that drops toward the creek dry since April
of 1995. But instead of descending, he floated
among the trees as though transformed
to warm breeze.
                        Then he was beside me.

I thought of all the things to avoid mentioning:
the state of poetry today, the fact that I am a Jew,
the mess virus has made of my body or how far
we are from the city. He was *an old man*
and this was *a dry month,* season, year. . . .
Best, I thought, not to quote him.
Even better not to amend his lines.

Mr. Eliot, we need to find the deep aquifer.

Especially at summer dusk, we have been lulled by
voices singing out of empty cisterns and exhausted wells.

Lulled by late darkness and the hope of deep mountain
snows next winter, dreams of extravagant melts
next spring followed by long rains that linger
at least through July. Now it is too late, the well
has all but died, *only rock and no water*
and the gravel road.

                           Who better to remind us
that the time has come to drill deep, to trace
the remote history of water down so that *time future*
does not *contain time present.*

                                 I meant so that cycles
cease to matter because we find ourselves down
where water always flows, the realm of ancient
floodwater freeing us from the desiccated surface
and its arid shallow layers.

                             Tom, we need a new well
and they charge by the foot!

                             For the first time
he turned to smile, the London banker knowing a sound
investment when he heard it. Before I could speak,
he was back where the pooled light had blazed,
afloat as though sailing on a hidden sea. He knew
his way around a small craft and the wind.
He knew his way home without markers.

Soon he began to fade. Or perhaps it was a trick
of light in air too sere to hold him there,
or the presence of my wife, mugs of tea in hand,
smiling at me in a way he only remembered
from late in his life, that second chance at love.

Polite as ever, he took himself to the edge
of the hill, looking down, looking away
over the valley shadowed now by an evergreen,
showing me the light, a shimmering vision
that may have been water, and drifted off.

DOWSING FOR JOY

The dowser says he can discover joy
as well as water or the whereabouts
of elk in hunting season. Unfurled wire
hangers and forked sticks nestle in a leather
quiver he carries up our gravel drive
until a fold of land calls him to the west.

In the woods he seems half his eighty years
and his pale blue eyes deepen to sapphire
as he gazes where the breeze disappears.
He says there are signs everywhere,
obvious things that most of us simply miss
like the scent of blooming lilies carried on air,
or hidden fields of force that call us home
when we can no longer bear to be alone.
What is music but waves plucked from the sky
and is color not light disturbed before the eye
can find it? He reminds us no one doubts
the fact that wild animals know weather
well enough to hide before a storm arrives.
Are we not animals too? The agitation of a boy
lost in the forest pulls like the moon on tides
if a dowser is tuned in, if he can ask
the right question at the right time and cast
his spirit before him into the dark.

He stops to stake a vein of water for the site
of our well and strings ribbon over limbs
to track its turnings. Something tells him
there is more to know here. Among the oak
and fir he whispers questions to the night
ahead and smiles first at me, then at my wife
as the wires in his fists cross to find us both.

THE FALL TERM

For my daughter

Scrub oak sways over a bank of yarrow
on our hillside, creaking in the warm wind
that has been gathering since yesterday.

It is too hot and dry for song sparrows
or the lazuli bunting that have been
so voluble since the middle of May.
But wind and hardwood make music enough
to cover the silence you leave behind.

Now sunlight is whipping the weeds to foam,
a trick of the eye and distracted mind
coming to rest at last. Remember, home
is not where you live but where you are loved.
We will bring a basket of dried yellow
and pink yarrow flowers to remind you.

NABOKOV, MIST

My mind has made colossal efforts to distinguish
the faintest of personal glimmers in the impersonal
darkness on both sides of my life.
  —VLADIMIR NABOKOV, *Speak, Memory*

At first I thought it was an elk,
only the antlers visible above
morning mist, moving in waltz
time as in a dream. Though it was
bodiless, I knew in the fluid
landscape of long-term illness
nothing was impossible. Not even
the late season butterflies I saw next,
Pine Whites like supple tendrils
of flaring mist torn loose to quiver
in a sudden crosswind.

Then the elk shedding mist
revealed itself as Nabokov,
heavy as in his *Lolita* years,
net raised, eager for one more capture.

I saw nothing could distract him
from his prey. He moved without
motion and in the shifting haze
was pure consciousness within
a twist of shadow, drifting due north.

He always meant to explore this far
into Oregon, following the movement
of blues across one more summer.
In June when I saw a male Spring Azure
pale among our blueberry bushes,
I thought of Nabokov coming to life
at the very sight. The same day,
my cane sunk in mud, I saw

a Common Blue settle on silky lupine
in the meadow and sensed a ghost
of silvery flight against the hill's fold.

But till now I could not allow myself
to believe Nabokov was here,
collecting specimens, fading in
and out of sight. Yet here
he was, an example of slow
adaptation to death, perhaps,
or miracle of the mind's endless life.
A leak of light from the deep
dark he never wished to accept,
Nabokov winks with his whole body.

As I watch him circle the cosmos,
the mist begins to lift. He does not
see me, but in the clarifying light
I understand that he notices everything
else. Yarrow ruffled by his passing.
A rufous hummingbird frenzied
and still before the purple foxglove,
yellow umbels of fennel feathering
as wind begins to rise, Sara Orangetips
bouncing in a sun-drenched cluster
of mustard. I wonder if these were
there before Nabokov saw them for me.
Yes his body says as it opens to emit
a streak of sun. *This is heaven.*

He leaves behind a tinge
of Russian sage, something blue
across the grass like a silhouette
of laughter. As though fresh
from the land without seasons,
a Red Admiral circles the last place
Nabokov appeared, its wings wide
against the memory of mist.